APJ Abdul Kalam —The Missile Man of India

Dr. APJ Abdul Kalam is one of the most distinguished scientist of India. He is a renowned professor, aeronautical engineer and the chancellor of the Indian Institute of Space Science and Technology (IIST).

Dr. APJ Abdul Kalam served as the 11th President of India from 2002 to 2007. He is often referred as 'People's President'. He is also popularly known as the 'Missile Man of India', because of his extraordinary contribution in the development of Ballistic Missile project and Space Rocket Technology. He also worked as a scientist in ISRO and DRDO. He was awarded with the Bharat Ratna—India's highest civilian honour in 1997.

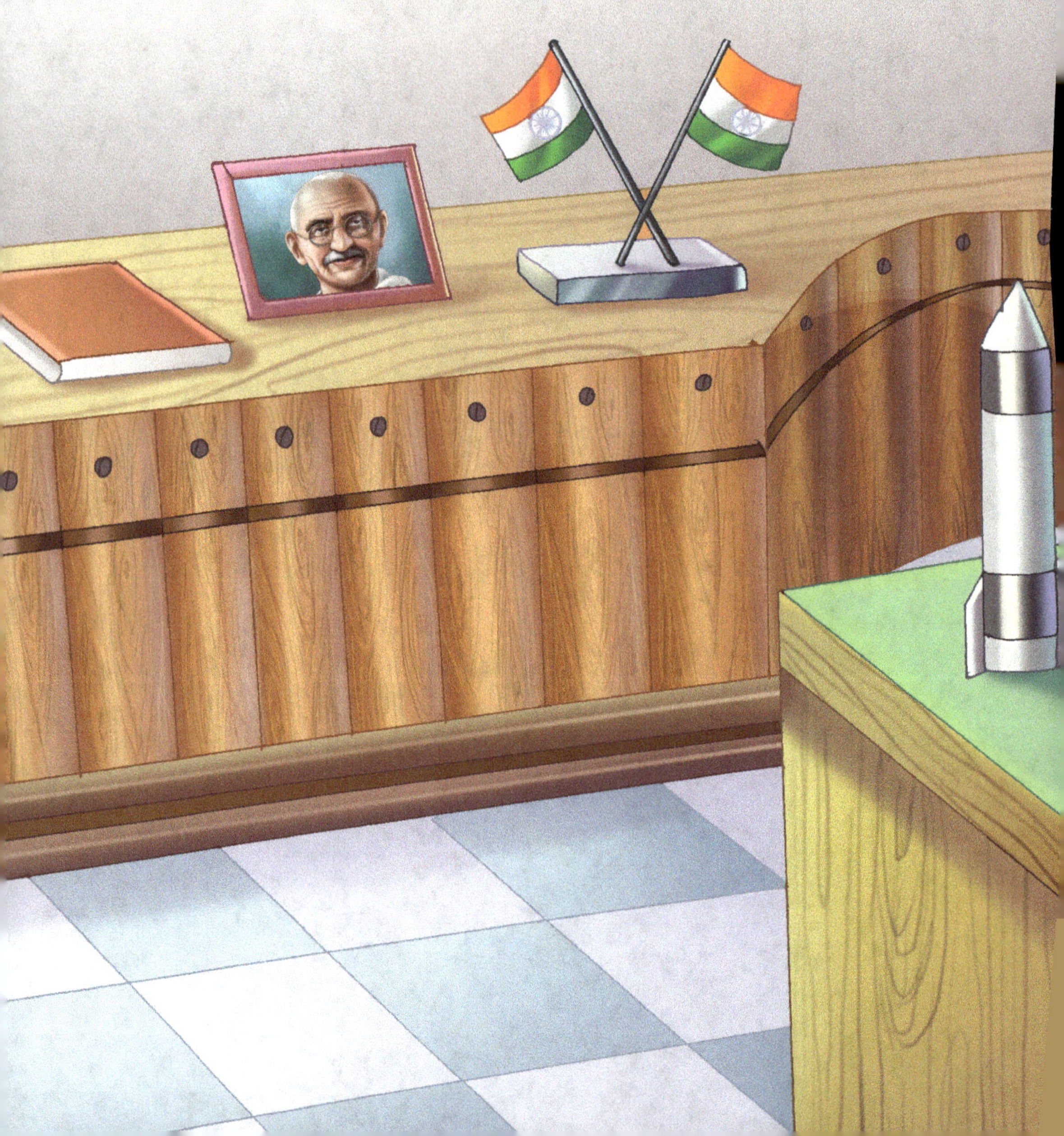

Birth and Early Years of Dr. Kalam's Life

Dr. APJ Abdul Kalam was born in Rameshwaram (in Tamilnadu) in a middle-class Muslim family on 15th October 1931. His father was Jainulabdeen and mother was Ashiamma. Dr. Kalam's full name is Avul Pakir Jainulabdeen. His father was a devout Muslim, who had good relations with the Rameshwaram temple priests. He used to rent his owned boats out to the local fishermen. He was a good friend of the Hindu religious leaders and school teachers of Rameshwaram.

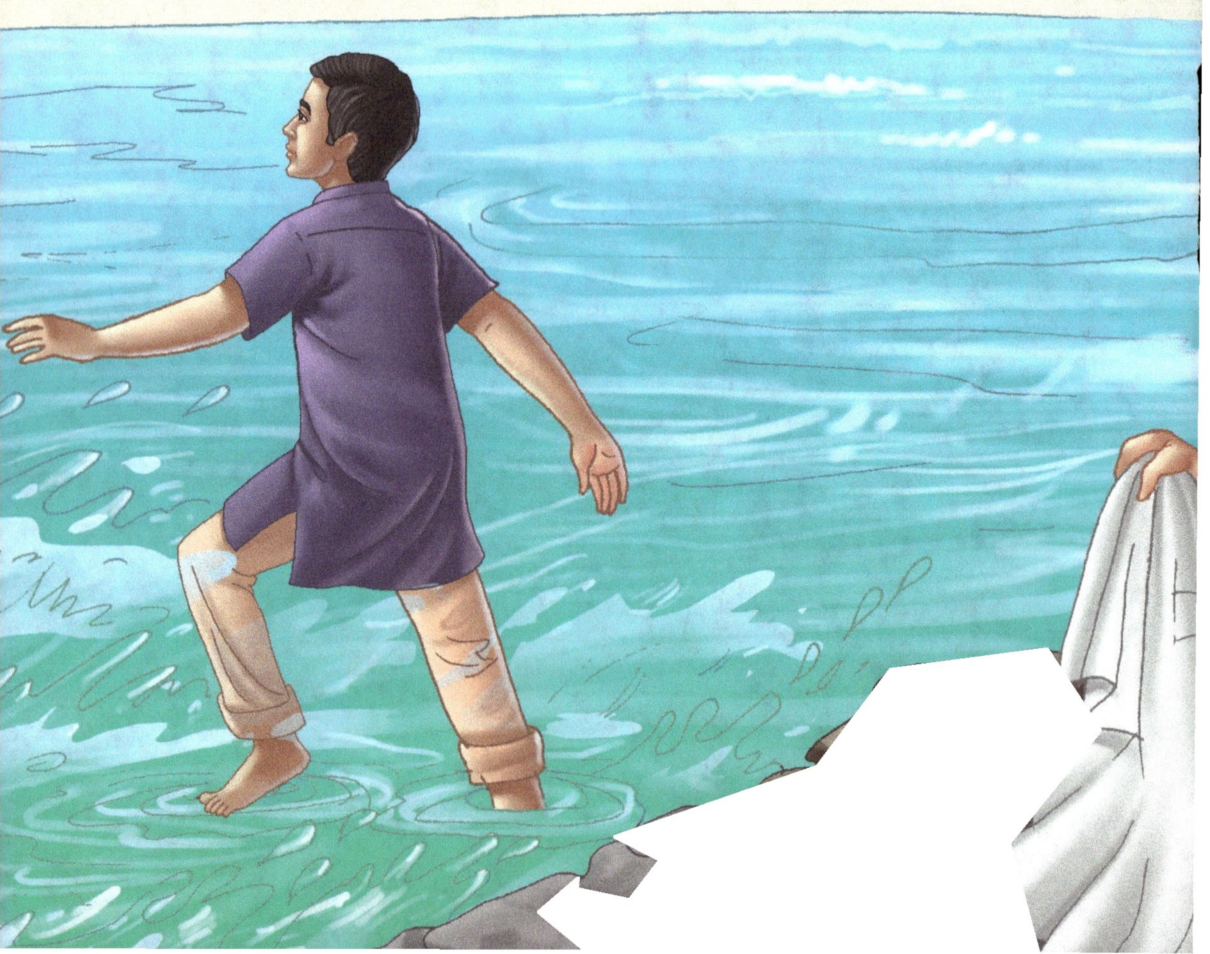

During his childhood, Dr. Kalam lived very close to the sea. He developed a great passion for nature and sea. He used to spend a lot of time watching the waves of sea. His mother influenced him to a great extent in developing his talents in music and writing poetry.

Dr. Kalam's parents led a very simple lifestyle. They imbibed good moral values in their children. Dr. Kalam became religious at a very young age. He reads 'Quran' and 'Bhagwat Geeta' daily and strictly follows vegetarian diet. Dr. Kalam devoted his entire life in doing research work.

Dr. Kalam spent most of his childhood in financial problems. His education began in a rural primary school at Rameshwaram. Later, he was shifted to Ramnathpuram Missionary School.

Dr. Kalam started working at a very early age. To bear the expenses of his education, he worked as a newspaper hawker.

His teachers, parents and others noticed his efforts and brilliance. Some of his teachers even came forward to help him.

After completing his school education in 1954, he took his graduation degree in Physics from St. Joseph College, Tiruchirapalli. In 1957, Kalam completed Bachelor of Engg. in Aerospace engineering from Madras Institute of Technology. Later he obtained advanced master and doctorate degrees in his respected field from the same institute.

Dr. Kalam's Professional Life

After completing his third year at MIT, he joined Hindustan Aeronautics Limited (HAL), Bangalore as a trainee and worked on the piston and turbine engines. In 1958, he came out of Hindustan Aeronautics Limited as a graduate.

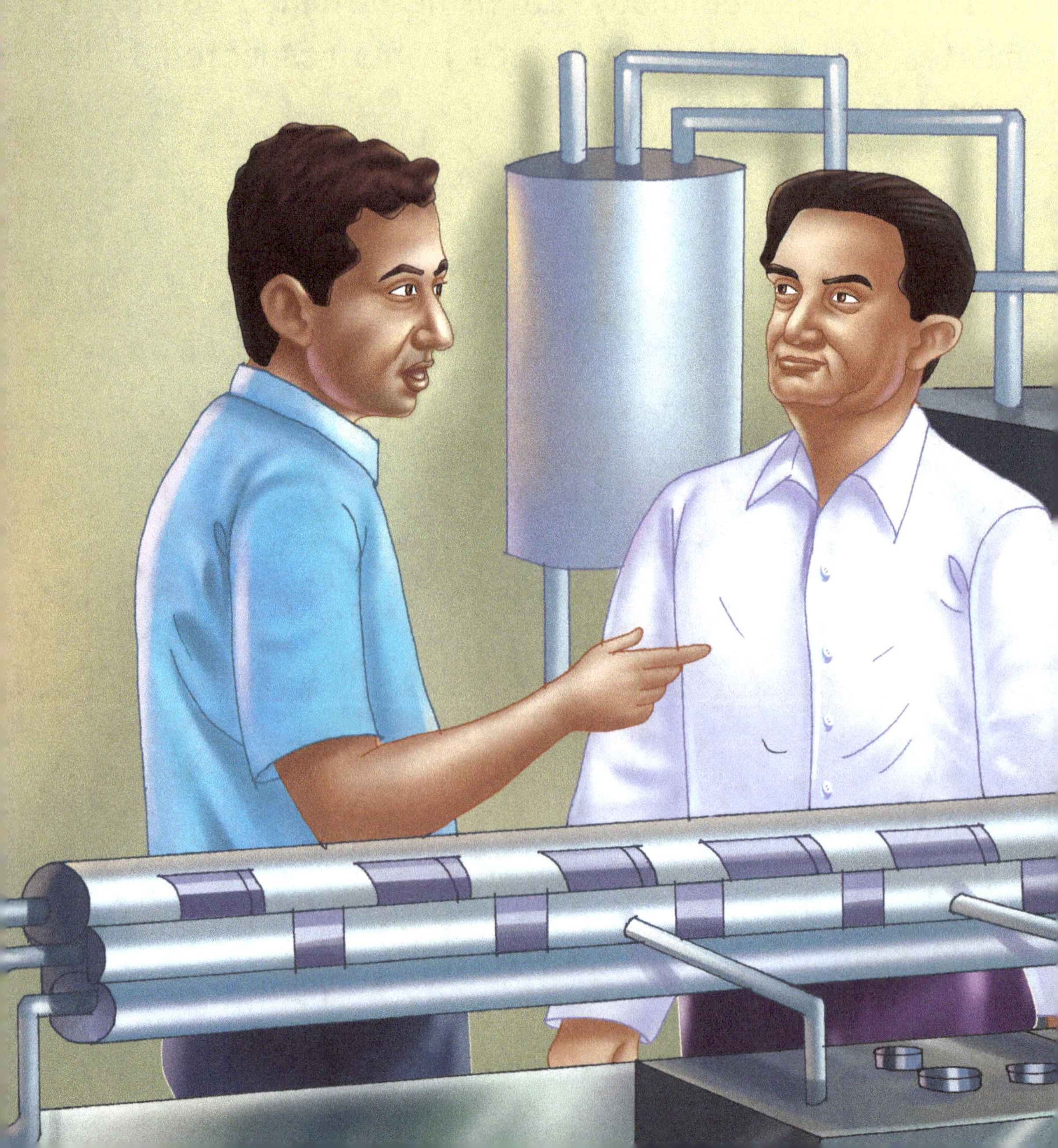

Thereafter, he got the opportunity to sewed at Indian Space Research Organisation (ISRO). After working on the several projects, he soon became a Project Director for India's first indigenous satellite launch vehicle (SLV-III) at Thumba.

The SLV-3 project was successful in placing Rohini—a scientific satellite—into orbit in July 1980 and was honoured with a Padma Bhushan in 1981. During this time, Dr. Kalam got to work with three great minds—Dr. Vikram Sarabhai, Professor Satish Dhawan and Dr. Brahm Prakash. He has also acknowledged these three people in his autobiography.

The second phase of Dr. Kalam's professional life started when he joined Defence Research Development Organisation (DRDO) in 1982. As Director of DRDO, he was entrusted with Integrated Guided Missile Development Program (IGMDP).

He played a major role in the development of many important Missiles like Nag, Akash, Trishul, Agni and Prithvi.

Three new laboratories for missile technologies were also developed during his tenure. His contributions in India's defence system are admirable.

Thereafter, Dr. Kalam worked as the Chairman of the Technology, Information, Forecasting and Assessment Council (TIFAC).

Dr. Kalam played a significant role in India's Pokharan-II nuclear test that was conducted in 1998.

In November 1999, Dr. Kalam was appointed as the Chief Scientific Advisor to the Govt. of India.
Later, in November 2001 he Joined Anna University at Chennai as a Professor of Technology and Societal Transformation.

Dr. Kalam—A Great Leader

When Dr. Kalam was working at the Rocket launching station in Thumba, there were around 70 scientists working under his leadership. To get success in their work and plan the scientists used to work for 12 to 18 hours daily. They could hardly spare any time for their families.

One day, a scientist came to Dr. Kalam and said, "Sir, I've promised my kids to take them to the exhibition going on in the town. So, I want to leave at 5.30 pm today, if you permit."

Dr. Kalam accepted his request and permitted him to leave at 5.30 pm. The scientist got engaged in his work. But when he finished the work it was almost 8.00 pm. He felt very bad that he had broken the promise given to his kids. Dr. Kalam was not in the office at that time.

In a Sad and tired mood, when he reached home he saw that his children were not at home. He asked to his wife about them. She replied, "Your Boss came here around 5.00 pm and took our kids for the exhibition."

The scientist was overwhelmed by the sweet gesture of his boss. Actually, Dr. Kalam saw that the scientist was engrossed in a very important work. And, he didn't want to disappoint the kids. So, he decided to take his children on his behalf for the exhibition.
Such an understanding and caring boss was Dr. Kalam.

Dr. Kalam as the President of India

The entire nation was surprised when the ruling NDA Government nominated Dr. Kalam—the famous scientist—as their candidate for the President elections. He won the election by huge margin and became the 11th President of India on 25th July 2002.

In his speech during the oath taking ceremony, Dr. Kalam said that we should be proud of our country, "In the last 50 years, India has made many achievements in the fields of food production, health sector, higher education, media & mass communication, information technology, science and defence. In spite of these advancements, a large population is still struggling with the problems like poverty, unemployment, diseases and lack of education."

Dr. Kalam expressed his vision to eradicate all the problems from the country and making it the strongest nation one day.

During his tenure, Dr. Kalam worked especially in the fields of science and education. He was remained as an approachable and humble President. He is very fond of the children and is always concerned for their development and welfare. He aimed to make India a scientifically strong nation and always tries to ignite the spark in the minds of Indian citizens.

Dr. Kalam has a multifaceted personality. Apart from being a great scientist, he is also interested in the field of arts and culture. He has written many books including his autobiography, 'Wings of Fire'. Some of his famous books are: 'Scientist to President', 'Ignited Minds: Unleashing the Power Within India', 'India 2020' etc.

He has also written Tamil poetry. Dr. Kalam is good at playing the Indian musical instrument 'Veena'.

Dr. Kalam has three visions. His first vision is freedom. He said that our country was ruled by many and remained dependent for a long period but we the Indians respect other's freedom, thus India has great values and culture.

Dr. Kalam's second vision is development. He said that though we have achieved a lot in the last few years, but we need to have more development, especially in the fields of education, science and technology.

His third vision is that India must be strong and emerge as a super power. It should stand up to the world and show its strength.

Dr. Kalam wants to make India an advanced and technologically developed nation. In his book, 'India 2020', he has mentioned an action plan to make India a knowledge superpower and a developed nation by the year 2020.

Dr. Kalam has been awarded with Bharat Ratna (1997), Padma Vibhushan (1990), Padma Bhushan (1981) and also received many more prestigious honours and awards.

He is presently the Chancellor of the Indian Institute of Space and Technology and also works as a professor at Anna University (Chennai) and as a visiting faculty in many academic and research institutes through out the country.

In May 2011, Dr. Kalam started a new mission for the Indian youth. 'What Can I Give Movement', is a unique mission to inculcate the Universal spirit of giving in the youth.

For years, Dr. Kalam has been inspiring many lives, especially the youth and children. He is the ocean of knowledge. We should draw inspiration from his life and must work to make India- a strongest nation.

On July 27, 2015, Dr. Kalam died after collapsing, while delivering a lecture at IIM, Shillong, Meghalaya. He was 83. The whole Nation mourned on his death, and paid homage, includes the President, the PM and other dignitaries, to him.

India's Hope: Narendra Modi

The land of Gujarat has produced many talented person who added to the glory of Gujarat and India. Shri Narendra Modi is also one such person, often addressed as the 'Gujarat's Development Man'. His life-story is full of struggles and hardships yet quite inspiring one as well. Nowadays the acronym of his name, 'Namo' (Narendra Modi) has become an inspiring mantra not only in the country but abroad as well for the majority of Indians.

Family and Childhood

Narendra Modi was born in Vadnagar, a small town in north Gujarat, in Mehsana district, on 17th Sept. 1950. His complete name is Narendra Damodardas Modi. His father's name is Damodardas Moolchand Modi and his mother is Hiraben Modi. His parents have six children and he is their third issue. His elder brothers are Somabhai and Amritbhai and two younger ones are Prahlad and Pankaj. His only younger sister is Vasantiben. His father, Damodardas, used to run a tea-stall near the office of a former Congress leader, Rasik Bhai Dave.

Financially his family was quite hard-pressed. Although Narendra Modi passed his childhood in utter penury, he never allowed the poverty influence his life in anyway. He would merrily swim in a river flowing nearby his home and enjoy his life in the company of his friends. Plucking off the raw mangoes from a closely mango-orchard was his favourite and the naughtiest prank.

Even at this age he had begun to appear quite thoughtful, and endowed with a foresight as well. What grieved most his young heart was the prevalent social evils like untouchability and injustice due to casteism. He equally abhorred discrimination practised against the women-folk. Depicting the agony of a Dalit woman he wrote a play called 'Peela Phool' (the yellow flower) in which he also played a role when it was staged.

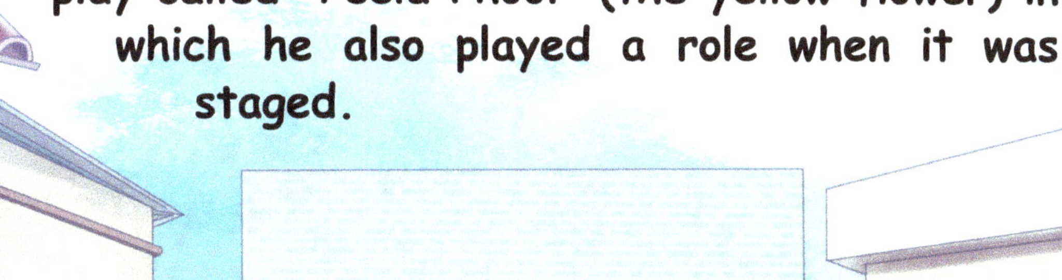

Education and Development

Child Narendra was admitted in the primary school of Vadnagar. Like an obedient son he regularly attended his classes. But he has an inborn urge to do something different, something extra-ordinary. He completed his education upto 10th class in the Bhagwataacharya Narayanaacharya Higher Secondary School. In 1967 Modi went to Visanagar for his intermediate education. Owing to his friendly attitude he developed a lot of friends among whom he was popularly known as 'ND' (the initials of his full name- Narendra Damodardas).

But whenever he saw his father working at the tea-stall, he felt quite disturbed. The longing to rise high and achieve something distinct was germinated at this very juncture. After his school hours he would invariably come to the tea-stall to help his father. Many a time he would himself accompany his father to the Vadnagar Railway Station to sell tea with him. At times he even sold water bottles and personally carried the oil-filled canisters of the oil companies. When he became young, the religious faith or Dharm had a distinct impact on him. For him Dharm meant social service and elimination of evils from the social ethos. He also emphasized on the spiritual aspect of Dharm. He keeps fast twice in a year during Navaratri festivals. He get internal strength from the fast.

Political Leadership

Right from his student life the quality of leadership had begun to show its effect which made him very popular. His readiness to help his fellow students in their hour of need and the capacity to guide them further honed up his leadership quality. Now he had started taking interest in the political happenings which not only inspired him but also made him become a source of inspiration for others. His belief was: 'he who thinks high and acts to fulfill his high aspirations eventually moves on the path of progress'.

His capacity to analyse the events and their consequences became his strength. When he faced any problem, first he would like to satisfy himself with its possible solution before guiding others. These qualities of him made him emerge as the leader of the Akhil Bhartiya Vidyarthi Parishad (ABVP).

He also served as the Pracharak of the RSS at various stations. But he had no desire to join politics. His only mission was spreading the thoughts and ideology of the Sangh. It was for this purpose, he joined 1974's 'Navnirman Andolan' , an agitation against corruption and came in the lime-light. In this phase, he got ample opportunity to learn the subtlety of politics. Meanwhile, continuing his studies, in 1980 he did his M.A. in Political Science from the University of Gujarat. In 1984, it was decided to include all the Sangh Pracharaks into the BJP. Looking at Modi's dedication, he was made a member of the BJP which heralded the beginning of his political career. In 1988, he was made the General Secretary of the State's BJP unit. Later on he was made the National Secretary of the BJP.

Tourism and Environment

Right from the childhood, Modi has abiding interest in Nature and environment. He loved swimming and could merrily swim across the Sharmishtha Lake, undaunted by its bubbling waves. He also loved visiting new places and seeing new sights. When he joined the RSS he got many more opportunities to behold Nature closely and understand its secrets. He would visit Ramakrishna Mission and Vivekananda Ashram in Almora. In 1972, he got an opportunity to travel picturesque Kangra as the Pracharak of RSS. He also wanted to stay for long in the Ramakrishna Mission in Belur Math but couldn't due to his other commitments. He specially visited Vivekananda Ashram of Almora perhaps in his attempt to follow the great seer's life principles. He also visited Kailash Mansarovar where he experienced much internal peace but he had to return soon owing to his father's demise.

Even before becoming the CM of Gujarat, Narendra Modi never neglected tourism because he knew the importance of environment and Nature. In 2001 when Modi took the charge as the CM, the State was recovering from the damages it underwent due to the massive earthquake. His government completed the Earthquake Rehabilitation Programme only in 8 months' time. The victims were properly rehabilitated and a campaign was launched to make people harvest rain water and meet their water demands. This campaign was admired globally and the World Bank awarded Gujarat with the 'Green Prize'.

Energy Power

After becoming the Gujarat CM, Gujarat's development became the new centre-point of Mr. Modi's ambitions. He stipulates the Panch Varsheeya Yojana (The Five Year Plan) which had five parts: Knowledge power, Energy power, Hydro power, People's power and the Fighting power (Rana-Shakti). This unprecedented plan proved very effective eventually and gave an impetus to Gujarat's progress which was based on Narendra Modi's original thinking and good management. All these powers encouraged the urban development plans in a tremendous way.

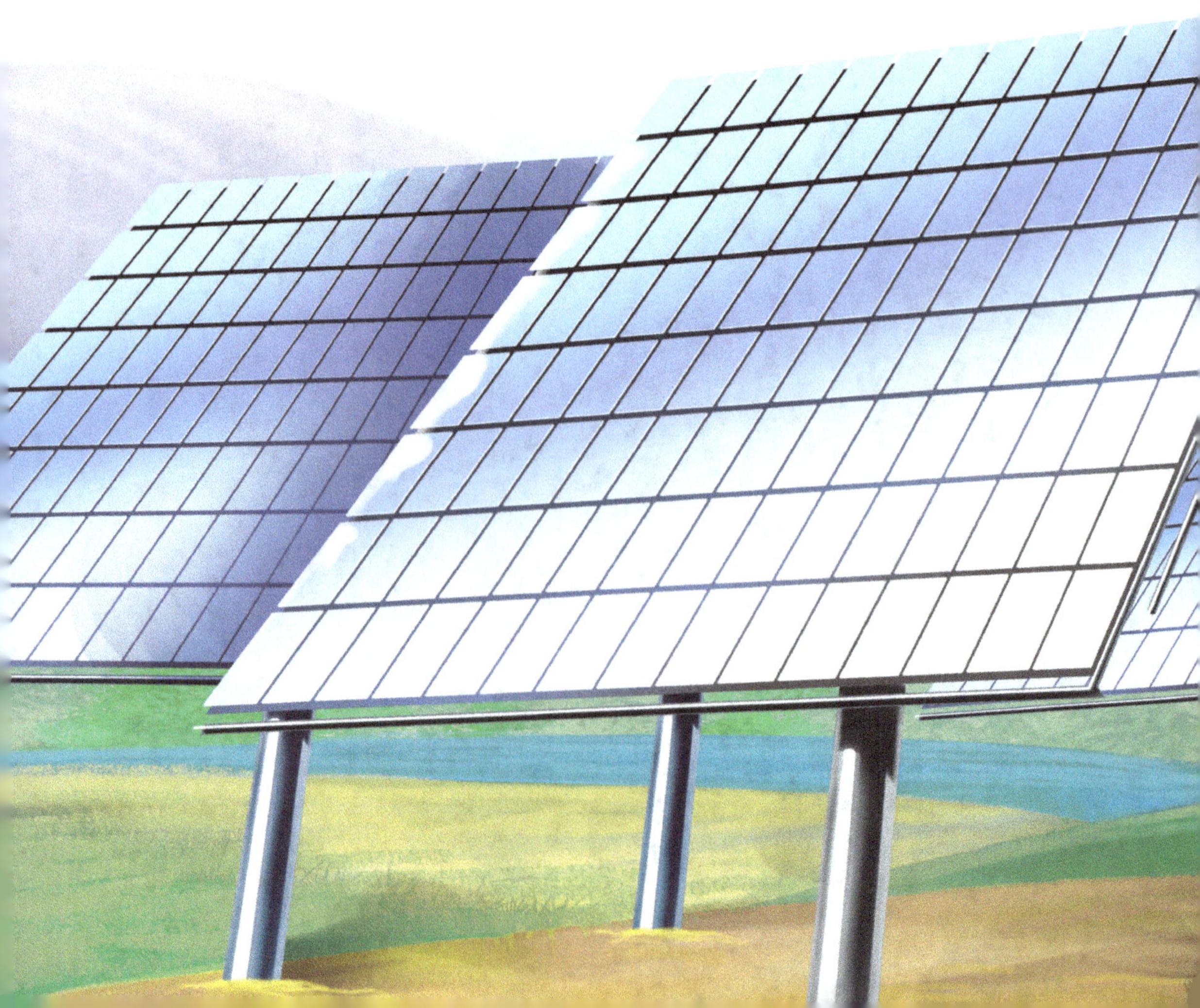

The knowledge power took care of education in the state. It was the basic power which further strengthened other powers. While the hydro-power gave new life to the famine-stricken Gujarat, the energy-power removed the poverty through providing much surplus power. Modi has not only succeeded in ushering an era of revolutionary development even in the corporate sector, he has succeeded in bringing out the white revolution. In fact these powers from the various sectors strengthened the very base of Modi's power. His energy rests on the people power of Gujarat.

Honour to Women

Narendra Modi always had much respect for women right from his early days. He has seen his mother getting exhausted with the domestic chores. His sister also helped her mother but still she needed an additional hand which was provided by the boy Modi. In order to lessen the domestic work's burden on his mother he always washed his own clothes and then himself ironed them. It was this sense of respect for the women which he depicted in his already referred play 'Peela Phool'. Most of the politicians regarded women as a mere support to men, although it is during Modi's regime that many women like Anandiben Patel, Smriti Irani, Sushma Swaraj could establish their distinct identity publicly.

He wanted to empower women of Gujarat which was possible only through right kind of education. In order to ensure every girl to be educated, a free-education campaign, called ' Kanya Kelwaani ' (girl education) was launched in every school. For ensuring the presence of all the tribal girls in their classrooms, their parents were promised 40 kilo cereals gift in return, and this scheme proved very effective. Rupees two thousands were given to every girl student for buying a cycle if their school was 3 kms. away from their home. Free bus service, computer-training were provided and security bonds worth 1000 rupees were also distributed. For providing training to open home-industry units, many kitchen gardens were opened. Some mobile training centres were also opened.

Nationalism

Under his leadership Gujarat progressed in every field, so much so that the famous international magazines like 'Time' and 'Economic' praised profusely his development model. His perception of 'Hinduism' inspires the people to create an ideal state. He doesn't believe in any kind of discrimination and gives equal importance to everybody—whether one be a peasant or an officer. His mind has no room for any kind of caste-based orthodoxy. He deems country or nation to be supreme and nothing is above it. For Narendra Modi nationalism means development of all communities. He emphasizes the integrity of the nation. His religion is only 'India First' and the only holy book is the Indian Constitution.

Patriotism

The seed of patriotism took the root in his heart when he was hardly six years old. He was greatly impressed by the former Congress leader, Rasikbhai Dave, near whose office his father ran his tea-stall. Narendra would regularly visit the office of his role-model. When Rasikbhai started his campaign to make Gujarat a separate state, Narendra joined it enthusiastically.

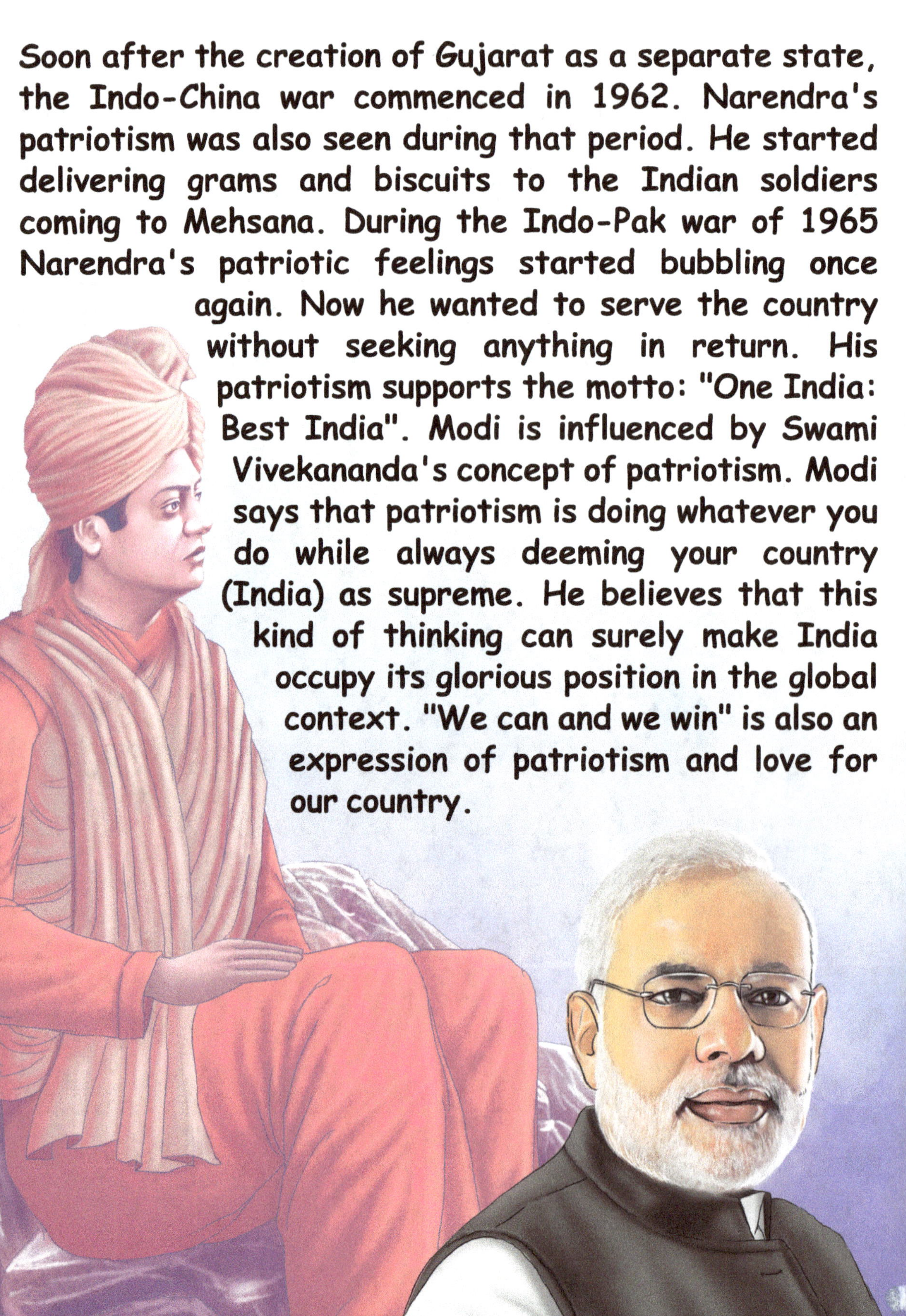

Soon after the creation of Gujarat as a separate state, the Indo-China war commenced in 1962. Narendra's patriotism was also seen during that period. He started delivering grams and biscuits to the Indian soldiers coming to Mehsana. During the Indo-Pak war of 1965 Narendra's patriotic feelings started bubbling once again. Now he wanted to serve the country without seeking anything in return. His patriotism supports the motto: "One India: Best India". Modi is influenced by Swami Vivekananda's concept of patriotism. Modi says that patriotism is doing whatever you do while always deeming your country (India) as supreme. He believes that this kind of thinking can surely make India occupy its glorious position in the global context. "We can and we win" is also an expression of patriotism and love for our country.

Role Model

So far the people of India had seen the persons of advanced age appearing as the leaders of the people. In such a common scenario, when Narendra Modi entered in the politics, his enchanting style of delivery of speech, dynamic personality and provoking thoughts gave a new ray of hope to the people of Gujarat. His impressive personality and fiery speeches received a warm welcome from the masses. He has become the role model of our country's youth.

Indian Development Schemes

The revolutionary development schemes launched and implemented by Prime Minister Shri Narendra Modi will help lead India towards the path of success by resolving economical conditions and reformation of various social issues. Because of this our country is being recognized world-over and their views are also changing towards our country.

Narendra Modi's Model of Development is highly praised across the nation. Introduction of revolutionary schemes such as Digital India, Clean India, Jan Dhan Yojna, Beti Padhao Beti Bachao, Make in India, Corruption Free India, and many more have changed the face of India. The country is being transformed into digital empowered society and knowledge economy. This initiative of e-governance and e-revolution aims at making all Government services accessible to the common man in his locality.

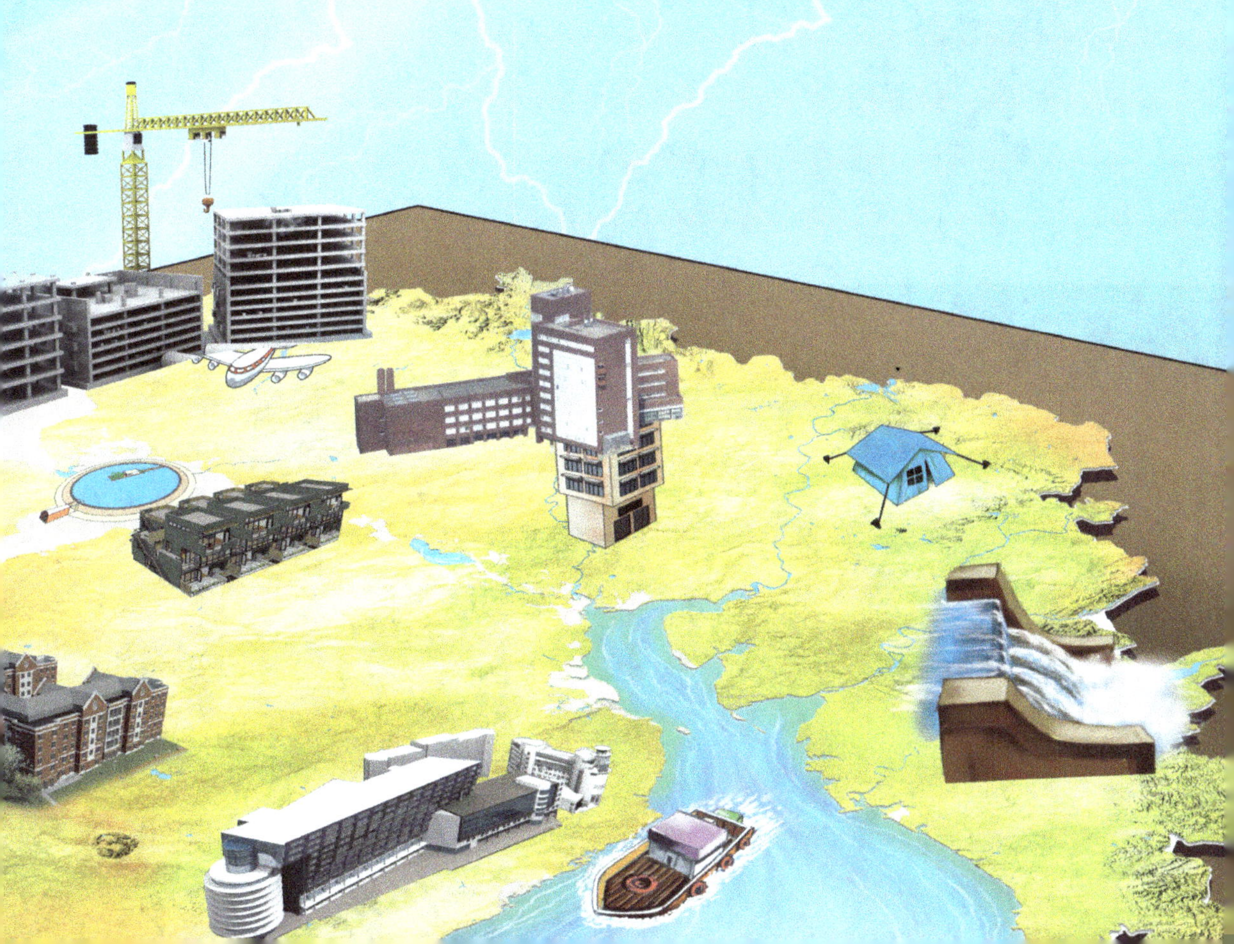

Pradhan Mantri Jan-Dhan Yojana (PMJDY), a National Mission for Financial Inclusion was introduced by the Prime Minister to ensure access to financial services, namely, Banking/ Savings & Deposit Accounts, Remittance, Credit, Insurance, Pension in an affordable manner. It was a grand success right from the day of inaugural. A record of 1.5 crore bank accounts were opened on the very first day across the country, the largest such exercise on a single day possibly anywhere in the world. So far, a total of more than 26 corers bank accounts are opened. Now common man will enjoy benefits of government schemes without having to go through endless waiting period or running from pillar to post. It will be reached directly to their accounts.

A nation which cannot ensure respect for its women, can never prosper. With the pet project launched by Prime Minister Shri Narender Modi "Beti bachao beti Padhao" (BBBP) Yojana (save daughter, educate daughter), countless girls and women have witnessed change in their lives. They are now making efforts towards fulfilling their dreams of being independent and having a career of their own.

India has the largest youth population in the world. With this in mind, Prime Minister Narendra Modi has taken a strong initiative named 'Make in India' project aiming at creating newer options and opportunities for employment in the country. In this way, our youth will develop his skills and contribute in the economy of the country.

India is an agrarian country. Our Pm Narendra Modi has introduced many new revolutionary schemes for the well being of agriculture sector in India. These plans have been introduced with an aim to ensure access to varied financial services including availability of basic savings bank account, remittances facility, access to need based credit, insurance and pension to the weaker sections, and low income groups. On the midnight of 9th November 2016, Shri Modi took a decision of demonetisation to curb the base of corruption in India. In this single move, he has attempted to tackle all major issues of the country including corruption, black money, terror funding, unemployment, and counterfeit currency in circulation. The impact of this great move has already started showing its results. All the schemes introduced by the Prime Minister are growth oriented and for the development of the country.